A BUCK DANNY
ADVENTURE

Sc____ Drawing: FRANCIS BERGÈSE
Work: FRÉDÉRIC BERGÈSE

NIGHT
OF THE SERPENT

The adventures of "Buck Danny" were created by Georges Troisfontaines, Victor Hubinon and Jean-Michel Charlier.

9th CINEBOOK
The 9th Art Publisher

Original title: Buck Danny 49 – La nuit du serpent
Original edition: © Dupuis, 2000 by Bergèse
www.dupuis.com
All rights reserved

English translation: © 2009 Cinebook Ltd

Translator: Jerome Saincantin
Lettering and text layout: Imadjinn sarl
Printed in Spain by Just Colour Graphic

This edition first published in Great Britain in 2009 by
CINEBOOK Ltd
56 Beech Avenue
Canterbury, Kent
CT4 7TA
www.cinebook.com

A CIP catalogue record for this book
is available from the British Library

ISBN 978-1-905460-85-4

9th CINEBOOK
The 9th Art Publisher

KUNSAN AIR BASE, SOUTH KOREA. THE OPERATIONS ROOM OF US AIR FORCE FIGHTER SQUADRON 35 IS STILL LIT UP, DESPITE THE LATE HOUR...

SORRY TO HAVE KEPT YOU SO LATE, CHUNG!

IT'S JUST A ROUTINE PATROL, BUT SINCE I HAVE TO TAKE OFF AT DAWN, I'D RATHER HAVE EVERYTHING SQUARED AWAY TONIGHT...

IT'S NO BOTHER, COLONEL MAXWELL. IT'S SUNDAY TOMORROW, AND MONDAY IS MY WEEKLY DAY OFF. I'LL HAVE PLENTY OF TIME TO CATCH UP ON MY REST.

GOOD! I'LL LET YOU FINISH EDITING THE SOFTWARE(*)... JUST LEAVE IT IN AN ENVELOPE ON MY DESK. THANKS, CHUNG. GOOD NIGHT!

GOOD NIGHT... AND GOOD FLIGHT, SIR!

NS.1A

(*) Navigation software containing the headings, heading changes, altitudes and timings to enter into the plane's onboard computer

MEANWHILE, 5600 MILES AWAY ON A SUNNY EARLY AFTERNOON, THE PARIS INTERNATIONAL AIR SHOW IS STARTING WITH THE AERIAL DEMONSTRATIONS OF THE WEEKEND...

GOSH! I WON'T MAKE IT... EJECT!... EJECT!

Francis Bergese

NS.1B

RHAA! SO FRUSTRATING!

THAT RASCAL OF A NORTH KOREAN MIG FIRED A MISSILE AT ME AT POINT-BLANK RANGE!... I TRIED TO BREAK AND DIVE, BUT IT DIDN'T WORK!

I'M TRYING THE MISSION AGAIN... IF I SUCCEED, I GET PROMOTED TO MAJOR!

HA! HA! NOW I UNDERSTAND WHY YOU'RE SO EAGER!... HEY, ONCE YOU'VE SUCCEEDED, CAN WE HAVE A TURN?... MAYBE I CAN MAKE COLONEL, AND BUCK WILL FINALLY GET HIS GENERAL'S STARS?!

LAUGH IT UP, FOOLS!... DOESN'T CHANGE THE FACT THAT WITH BOTH MY ACTUAL PROGRESS ON THE F-22 AND MY VIRTUAL WORK ON THE COMPUTER, I USE THE FULL POTENTIAL OF THE MACHINE BETTER THAN YOU AND PASSED YOU IN TRAINING!

THE LOCKHEED-MARTIN F-22 RAPTOR CURRENTLY ON DISPLAY IS ONE OF FOUR PRE-PRODUCTION AIRCRAFT PRESENTED HERE THAT WE WILL SEE FLYING FORMATION TOMORROW...

FOR THE MOMENT, YOU'D BE BETTER OFF WORKING ON YOUR FORMATION FLYING RATHER THAN PRACTICING COMBAT!

IN THIS SIMULATOR, YOU'RE ALWAYS THE LEADER!

LEADER AND SOON MAJOR!... IS THAT ALL!... SAY, THIS LAPTOP SEEMS TO HOLD MOST OF YOUR LIFELONG DREAMS, DOESN'T IT!

HEATHEN! YOU UNCULTURED, NEUROPSYCHOLOGICAL INDIGENT!

THE F-22, OF WHICH THERE ARE CURRENTLY ONLY NINE, INCLUDING TWO PROTOTYPES, IS BEING EVALUATED BY THE US AIR FORCE. THIS ONE IS FLOWN BY MAJOR DICK JACKSON, WHOM WE WILL SEE AGAIN TOMORROW AS NUMBER THREE OF THE FORMATION...

THE THREE OTHER PILOTS OF THESE AIRCRAFT ARE COLONEL BUCK DANNY, MAJOR JERRY TUMBLER AND CAPTAIN SONNY TUCKSON, WHO ARE FOR TODAY SIMPLE SPECTATORS...

... AND IT FEELS GOOD!

NOT TO ME!

THIS PLANE IS CLASSIFIED AS STEALTHY, WHICH MEANS IT IS DIFFICULT TO DETECT ON RADAR. AS YOU MAY HAVE NOTICED, IT IS ALSO RATHER QUIET, WHICH CONTRIBUTES TO ITS DISCRETION. ITS TWIN JET ENGINES, WITH A COMBINED THRUST OF 34 TONS, ARE EQUIPPED WITH A THRUST VECTORING SYSTEM THAT ALLOWS FOR EXTREMELY TIGHT MANOEUVRING, AS YOU CAN SEE FOR YOURSELVES...

THE INFRARED SIGNATURE OF ITS ENGINES WAS ALSO GREATLY REDUCED COMPARED TO CONVENTIONAL FIGHTERS. ANOTHER CHARACTERISTIC: THE "RAPTOR" CAN REACH SUPERSONIC SPEED WITHOUT THE USE OF AFTERBURNERS(*)...

(*) Component increasing the thrust of a jet engine by injecting fuel directly into the jet pipe downstream of the turbine

THE SAME EVENING, IN A GREAT HOTEL IN PARIS...

SO, SONNY, NO CRITICISMS ABOUT MY SHOW?

SNAILS ARE TASTY... YOU SHOULD TRY SOME!... EH? YOUR SHOW?... OH, YEAH, IT WAS GREAT!

YEAH, RIGHT! HE HAD HIS NOSE GLUED TO HIS COMPUTER SCREEN THE WHOLE TIME!

CAPTAIN TUCKSON OWNS A VIRTUAL F-22 AND IS ALREADY UP TO ADVANCED AIR COMBAT! DID YOU KNOW HE'LL SOON BE PROMOTED TO VIRTUAL MAJOR?

KEEP LAUGHING, YOU BONEHEADED TWERP!... BUT ONCE WE GET TO WEAPONS TRAINING, I'LL BE WELL AHEAD OF YOU!

NS.3A

WELL, THAT'LL BE A CHANGE!... LAST WEEK DURING A TRAINING FLIGHT, I GOT ON HIS HIGH SIX WHILE FLYING A SIMPLE F-16... HE DIDN'T BRAG ABOUT THAT ONE!

YEAH, BUT FIRST OF ALL YOU HAD THE POSITION GOING FOR YOU, AND THEN I USED MY VECTORED THRUST TOO EARLY...

ER... WHO ORDERED THE FROG LEGS...?

HERE! WE DID!

YES! LET THERE BE FROG LEGS APLENTY!

BUT THERE...

?

HOOO!

PLAF

THEY SHOULD HAVE HAD THE SNAILS... THEY DON'T JUMP!

NS.3B

ON THIS EARLY SUNDAY MORNING, SOUTH OF THE DEMILITARIZED ZONE SEPARATING THE TWO KOREAS(*), LIEUTENANT-COLONEL MAX MAXWELL, IN HIS F-16C "FALCON," IS FLYING THE ROUTINE PATROL PREPARED THE NIGHT BEFORE...

DEAD CALM... NOTHING ON THE RADAR, AND I CAN'T SEE ANYTHING SPECIAL TO REPORT EITHER...

(*) See textbox at the bottom of the page.

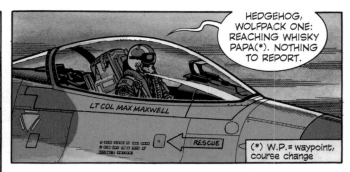

HEDGEHOG, WOLFPACK ONE: REACHING WHISKY PAPA(*). NOTHING TO REPORT.

LT COL MAX MAXWELL

RESCUE

(*) W.P. = waypoint, course change

MEANWHILE, IN PARIS...

SLEEP TIGHT, CHAPS!... THE BUS TO LE BOURGET AIRFIELD LEAVES THE HOTEL AT TEN—DON'T MISS IT!... PILOTS' BRIEFING IS AT ELEVEN.

NS.4A

WHILE THE SUN RISES IN KOREA, MAXWELL CONTINUES HIS MONOTONOUS PATROL FLIGHT ALONG THE BORDER...

MY RWR(*) IS TELLING ME A TRACKING RADAR ON MY TWO O'CLOCK HAS TAGGED ME... BAH!... I'LL NOTE THE TIME AND LOCATION, PER STANDING ORDERS...

(*) Radar Warning Receiver—radar detector

UH?... WHAT'S THAT OVER THERE?! IT'S AS IF THE SUN WAS BEING REFLECTED IN FLASHES STRONGLY ON A CANOPY...

IT'S BLINKING LIKE MORSE CODE... STRANGE... IT'S...

LT COL MAX MAXWELL

RESCUE

HAAAA!

LT COL MAX MAXWELL

RESCUE

NS.4B

Since the end of the Second World War, Korea has been split in two along the 38th parallel. In the North is the People's Republic, backed by China and the USSR—until the latter disintegrated—and ruled with an iron fist by dictator Kim Il Sung, then by his son Kim Jong Il, it remains a hard-line Communist country. To the South is the Democratic Republic, backed by the USA. The two countries are separated by a Demilitarized Zone (called DMZ) that runs from the Yellow Sea to the Sea of Japan in a 2.5 mile-wide band, along which on both sides sizeable forces are massed, ready to face a surprise invasion by the other side's army. To this Demilitarized Zone is added a "No Fly Zone," the width of which varies between three and nine miles, depending on the ground features chosen to define it.

AAAH! I CAN'T SEE ANYTHING!... JUST THIS RED!

HEDGEHOG, WOLFPACK ONE... I... I'VE BEEN BLINDED BY AN INTENSE... RED LIGHT!

WOLFPACK ONE, THIS IS HEDGEHOG... DID YOU GET A FIX ON THE LOCATION?

I GOT AN APPROXIMATE FIX... I SAW SOME FLASHES OF LIGHT ABOUT 12 MILES ON MY TWO O'CLOCK... THE SAME DIRECTION AS A RADAR THAT HAD JUST LIT UP... THEN THERE WAS THIS VIOLENT RED LIGHT! I STILL CAN'T SEE ANYTHING!

ABORT THE MISSION, WOLFPACK!... SWITCH TO WHISKY PAPA ZERO(1) AND LET YOUR A.P.(2) BRING YOU BACK!

WHISKY PAPA ZERO... I'M HEADING HOME... LET'S HOPE MY SIGHT WILL BE BACK BEFORE I REACH THE BASE...

(1) Waypoint Zero is located on the geographical coordinates of the starting base. (2) Autopilot

IF YOU'RE NOT ABLE TO LAND BY THEN, WE'LL DIRECT YOU TOWARDS THE SEA WHERE YOU CAN EJECT.

I WAS FLYING TOWARDS WAYPOINT 6... I HAD THREE MORE TO GO... SO, BY CLICKING FOUR TIMES, I SHOULD GET BACK TO WAYPOINT 0...

BUT LESS THAN A MINUTE LATER ...

HEY, WOLFPACK! THIS IS HEDGEHOG! WHAT ARE YOU DOING?... MY SCREEN HAS YOU HEADING DUE NORTH!

WHAT?... BUT THAT'S IMPOSSIBLE! I ENTERED WHISKY PAPA ZERO, WHICH SHOULD BE SENDING ME DUE SOUTH!... AND IF I HAD MISCOUNTED CLICKS, I SHOULD BE GOING EITHER EAST OR WEST, BUT NOT NORTH IN ANY CASE!

YOU'RE CROSSING THE DMZ!... TURN BACK! TURN BACK!

THIS IS CHECKPOINT 53! HOTDOG ALERT!... HOTDOG ALERT!

NS.5A

GOOD GRIEF!... "HOTDOG ALERT"! THAT'S A SIGNAL FROM THE BORDER SENTRIES... I'M ACTUALLY CROSSING THE DEMILITARIZED ZONE!... WHAT'S GOING ON?!...

YOUR RADAR RETURN IS STARTING TO BLINK, WOLFPACK... YOU MUST BE SERIOUSLY CLOSE TO THE GROUND!... PULL UP AND TURN BACK!

LT COL MAX MAXWELL

RESCUE

I DON'T HAVE YOU ON MY SCREEN ANYMORE, WOLFPACK... PULL UP!

I'M TURNING THE AP OFF AND PULLING ON THE STICK... THEN I'LL SELECT MY PREVIOUS WAYPOINT, NUMBER 5, SO THE PLANE WILL TAKE ME BACK TO WHERE I WAS BEFORE— THE INCIDENT...

WP 8thFW

I'VE GOT YOU AGAIN, WOLFPACK... DID YOU TURN AROUND?... YOU'RE NOW OVER 10 MILES BEYOND OUR LINES!

I'M SWITCHING ON THE AP ON WHISKY PAPA 5, WHICH SHOULD BRING ME BACK SOUTH AT MY CRUISING ALTITUDE OF 8000 FEET.

IT'S NOT WORKING, WOLFPACK! YOU'RE BACK ON A NORTH HEADING!

WHAT?! I... I'LL TRY THE OTHER WAYPOINTS!

Francis Bergese

NS.5B

I'M CYCLING THROUGH ALL MY WAYPOINTS, BUT THE PLANE ISN'T MOVING AN INCH!

THAT'S UNBELIE‐VABLE!

I'M GETTING THE AUDIO WARNING FOR A FIRE-CONTROL RADAR! I'M GONNA BE LIT UP LIKE A CHRISTMAS TREE IN A SECOND!... WHAT THE HECK! WHAT IS GOING ON WITH THIS NAVIGATION SYSTEM?!

BEEP BEEP BEEP BEEP BEEP BEEP BEEP BEEP BEEP BEEP

YOUR RETURN IS BLINKING OFF. YOU'RE LOSING ALTITUDE AGAIN!

TRY TO TURN AND CLIMB FOR ABOUT 10 SECONDS, THEN TURN ON YOUR AP IN PRIMARY MODE(*). THEN WE'LL GIVE YOU THE NECESSARY CORRECTIONS TO BRING YOU BACK SOUTH. ACKNOWLEDGE, WOLFPACK.

(*) The autopilot simply keeps to the heading and altitude at the time it is turned on.

ROGER... I'M TURNING AND CLIMBING...!... OH, NO! I'M HIT! THEY'RE USING THEIR GUNS!... I CAN'T CONTROL... EJECTING... EJECTING!

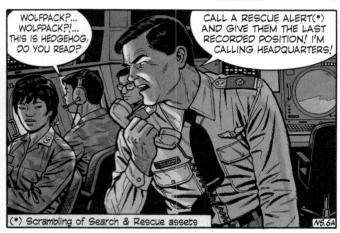

WOLFPACK?... WOLFPACK?!... THIS IS HEDGEHOG, DO YOU READ?

CALL A RESCUE ALERT(*) AND GIVE THEM THE LAST RECORDED POSITION! I'M CALLING HEADQUARTERS!

(*) Scrambling of Search & Rescue assets   NS.6A

I CAN'T BE TOO HIGH... AND I DON'T KNOW WHAT KIND OF TERRAIN I CAN EXPECT...

OUCH!

THE SLOPE IS GETTING STEEPER... I'M SLIDING!...

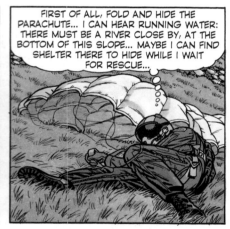

FIRST OF ALL, FOLD AND HIDE THE PARACHUTE... I CAN HEAR RUNNING WATER: THERE MUST BE A RIVER CLOSE BY, AT THE BOTTOM OF THIS SLOPE... MAYBE I CAN FIND SHELTER THERE TO HIDE WHILE I WAIT FOR RESCUE...

HAAAA!

NS.6B

PLASH

HRA!

GLUB!

I'M IN A CANAL—THE WALLS ARE VERTICAL AND MADE OF CONCRETE... NOT A SINGLE OUT-CROPPING TO HANG ON TO!

FOR SEVERAL MINUTES THAT SEEM LIKE AN ETERNITY, MAXWELL IS ROLLED AND SHAKEN BY THE CURRENT, BOUNCING FROM ONE WALL TO THE OTHER...

GOOD GRIEF! WHEN IS THIS HELLISH RIDE GOING TO END?

THE CURRENT IS WEAKENING... MY FEET CAN TOUCH THE BOTTOM, BUT IT'S SLIPPERY... AND STILL NOTHING TO GRAB ON!

THERE!... I HOPE I CAN HOLD ON!

PHEW!

BONG

OUCH!

COULD MY SIGHT BE COMING BACK?... I THINK I CAN MAKE OUT SOME LIGHT AND SHADOWS...

I'M UNDER A BRIDGE... I MIGHT AS WELL STAY HERE AND HOPE IT'S A GOOD HIDING SPOT. I'LL GET OUT OF COVER EVERY ONCE IN A WHILE TO TURN ON MY BEACON(*)... A RESCUE OPERATION WILL PROBABLY BE ORGANISED TO GET ME OUT OF HERE, BUT MOST LIKELY NOT UNTIL DARK.

(*) Small emitter allowing Search & Rescue teams to locate downed pilots

PARIS, AROUND NINE HOURS LATER...

CLICK IT'S EIGHT O'CLOCK. THE NEWS WITH CHRISTIAN BERGER... GOOD MORNING... INCIDENT IN KOREA: A US JET SHOT DOWN OVER NORTH KOREA...

THE NORTH KOREAN GOVERNMENT HAS ANNOUNCED THAT ITS AIR DEFENCE FORCES SHOT DOWN A US AIR FORCE F-16 THAT HAD FLOWN OVER 12 MILES INTO ITS TERRITORY...

THE OFFICIAL PRESS AGENCY OF THE PEOPLE'S REPUBLIC OF KOREA IS PROVIDING THE WORLD'S MEDIA WITH PICTURE OF THE PLANE'S WRECKAGE...

... NEXT TO WHICH HAS BEEN DEPOSITED THE PILOT'S EJECTOR SEAT. ACCORDING TO THE PRESS RELEASE, THE LATTER WAS CAPTURED SHORTLY AFTER HIS EJECTION, BUT NO PICTURES HAVE BEEN PROVIDED TO CONFIRM THIS STATEMENT...

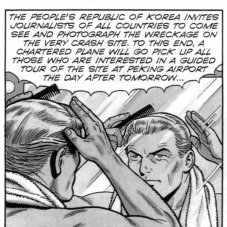

THE PEOPLE'S REPUBLIC OF KOREA INVITES JOURNALISTS OF ALL COUNTRIES TO COME SEE AND PHOTOGRAPH THE WRECKAGE ON THE VERY CRASH SITE. TO THIS END, A CHARTERED PLANE WILL GO PICK UP ALL THOSE WHO ARE INTERESTED IN A GUIDED TOUR OF THE SITE AT PEKING AIRPORT THE DAY AFTER TOMORROW...

THEY WILL ALSO BE ABLE TO MEET, QUOTE: "THE SHARPSHOOTING NAM PHUENG WHO, WITH A SINGLE BURST OF HIS 23MM GUN, BROUGHT DOWN THIS SPY PLANE, OFFERING ANOTHER PROOF OF THE UNSTOPPABLE ARROGANCE OF AMERICAN IMPERIALISM!"

IT SEEMS THAT WITH THIS INCIDENT NORTH KOREA HAS THE OPPORTUNITY TO STRIKE A DECISIVE MEDIA BLOW BY POSITIONING ITSELF, ONCE AGAIN, AS THE VICTIM OF AN AMERICAN-SOUTH KOREAN CONSPIRACY...

FROM THE AMERICAN SIDE, WE STILL HAVEN'T SEEN ANY OFFICIAL REACTION. A SPOKESPERSON FOR THE US AIR FORCE SAID THAT TO HIS KNOWLEDGE NO PLANE HAD BEEN LISTED AS MISSING AND THAT IT WAS PROBABLY ONE OF THOSE SCHEMES SO CUSTOMARY FROM NORTH KOREA...

HEADQUARTERS OF PACIFIC AIR FORCES, HICKAM AIR FORCE BASE, HAWAII...

WHERE DO WE STAND, COLONEL PERKINS?

A SPECIAL OPERATIONS "PAVE LOW" HELICOPTER SHOULD BE LEAVING KADENA(1) AT THIS MOMENT, HEADING TO OSAN TO BE AVAILABLE FOR THE EXTRACTION OF COLONEL MAXWELL. THE RC-135(2) HAS BEEN ON SITE FOR SEVERAL HOURS ALREADY...

HOW ARE THINGS LOOKING?

(1) Large US Air Force base on the island of Okinawa, south of Japan.
(2) Boeing 707 specialised in electronic surveillance.

SHORT TRANSMISSIONS FROM MAXWELL'S BEACON HAVE BEEN RECEIVED SEVERAL TIMES, AND A BRIEF DIALOGUE WAS ESTABLISHED. TO THE QUESTIONS FROM THE RC-135, THE PILOT GAVE YES OR NO ANSWERS. IT DIDN'T ALLOW US TO LOCATE HIM PRECISELY, BUT NEITHER WILL THOSE WHO ARE TRYING TO CAPTURE HIM!...

WHAT DO WE KNOW?

HE'S STILL BLIND BUT ABLE-BODIED. HE HAS YET TO BE THREATENED BY TROOP PROXIMITY. WE ASKED HIM TO TRANSMIT ONLY IN A DESPERATE SITUATION, OR AT THE MOMENT WE SIGNAL HIM THE ARRIVAL OF THE RESCUE TEAM SO WE CAN LOCATE HIM PRECISELY.

ABOUT TWO HOURS LATER, ON THE NORTH HIGHWAY IN THE OUTSKIRTS OF PARIS...

WHAT DO YOU THINK OF THIS KOREAN BUSINESS, BUCK?

TRANSPORTS GENDROT 26750 BEDEVILLE

NS 9A

GENERAL SCOTT... ARE YOU FLYING TO KADENA NOW?

AFFIRMATIVE. THAT'S WHERE THE PENTAGON(*) WILL LET ME KNOW IF I MUST LAUNCH OPERATION SNEAKY SERPENT!...

(*) Headquarters of the US Armed Forces, located near Washington DC

IT DOESN'T MAKE SENSE... THE PICTURES AND THE INVITATION TO THE WORLD'S PRESS WOULD LEAD ME TO THINK THAT THE INCIDENT IS REAL. BUT THE BORDER IS MADE PERFECTLY VISIBLE FROM THE SKY... AND WITH MODERN NAVIGATION SYSTEMS, YOU SIMPLY CANNOT GET LOST ANYMORE!

I CAN ONLY SEE TWO POSSIBILITIES: TEMPORARY DIZZINESS OF THE PILOT, OR A SECRET MISSION... BUT BOTH SEEM TO ME EQUALLY UNLIKELY!

IN SHORT, ANOTHER PIECE OF BAD BUSINESS THAT'S GOING TO RATCHET THE TENSION BETWEEN THE TWO KOREAS UP A GOOD-SIZED NOTCH!...

A LITTLE WHILE LATER, ON A PARKING AREA OF DUGNY MILITARY BASE, ON THE OTHER SIDE OF LE BOURGET'S MAIN RUNWAY...

EVERYTHING ALL RIGHT, JIM?

EVERYTHING OKAY, SIR!

U.S. AIR FORCE

OUR BEAUTIES HAVE BEEN POLISHED LIKE WE'LL PROBABLY NEVER HAVE THE TIME TO DO AGAIN!

WHAT THE HECK IS THIS?!

NS9B

I MUST SPEAK WITH YOU IN PRIVATE, COLONEL. WOULD YOU PLEASE CLIMB INTO THE CAR?

?!... THEY'RE TAKING OUR BUCK AWAY NOW!

THAT COLONEL AND HIS UNDERTAKER AIRS, DRIVING UP IN THAT HEARSE, ARE GIVING ME A BAD FEELING!

FIVE MINUTES LATER...

WHAT'S GOING ON, BOSS?

CHANGES IN THE PROGRAM... COME WITH ME INTO THE "BLACKHAWK."

THESE ARE MISSION ORDERS FOR THE FOUR OF US: AFTER TODAY'S SHOW, WE WON'T BE LANDING HERE... WE HEAD FOR RYAD, SAUDI ARABIA.

AND THAT TUBE ?!...

THE MAPS TO PREPARE THE FLIGHT, DUMMY!

THE EMBASSY WILL TAKE CARE OF GETTING OUR LUGGAGE FROM THE HOTEL AND SENDING IT OVER. STAY QUIET ABOUT THIS EARLY DEPARTURE.

IT'S ALMOST 3100 MILES BETWEEN HERE AND RYAD... FOR OUR AERIAL DEMONSTRATION, WE ONLY HAVE A QUARTER OF A FULL FUEL LOAD(1)...

AFTER ONE HOUR AND 15 MINUTES AT ECONOMY CRUISE SPEED, WE'LL REACH THE ADRIATIC, WHERE WE'LL RENDEZVOUS WITH A KC-135(2)...

(1) For long-distance flight, the F-22 can be equipped with extra fuel pods inside its weapon compartment. (2) Tanker Boeing

THEN, USING SUPERCRUISE(*) WHEN ABOVE WATER, THE TOTAL FLIGHT TIME SHOULDN'T BE OVER FIVE HOURS.

(*) The F-22 can, at high altitude, maintain a supersonic cruise speed of approximately 1000 mph.

WE'LL HAVE TO WARN THE AIR SHOW ORGANISATION THAT WE WON'T BE LANDING AFTER OUR PRESENTATION...

OUR EMBASSY IS TAKING CARE OF IT. ALL WE HAVE TO DO IS TO PREPARE THE NAVIGATION AND GO GET SOMETHING TO EAT AT THE LOCKHEED-MARTIN BUNGALOW.

AT THE SAME INSTANT IN KOREA, ALONG THE NO-FLY ZONE...

ALL RIGHT... THEY'RE STILL LOOKING FOR HIM!

WE'VE INTERCEPTED COMMUNICATIONS FROM THE TROOPS IN THAT AREA — WHAT ARE THEY SAYING, CHIL?

TWO SEARCH PARTIES JUST RENDEZVOUSED NEAR THE TAN-WU RIVER. THEY'RE REPORTING TO THEIR LEADERSHIP THAT THEY FOUND NOTHING!

OSAN USAF BASE, NEAR THE BORDER, AS NIGHT FALLS.

GENTLEMEN... CONTRARY TO WHAT PRESS AGENCIES ARE ANNOUNCING, LIEUTENANT-COLONEL MAXWELL HASN'T BEEN CAPTURED. HE'S BEEN USING HIS BEACON SPORADI-CALLY, FOR VERY BRIEF AND NON-VERBAL TRANSMISSIONS TO AVOID BEING DETECTED...

HE MUST HAVE FOUND AN EXCELLENT HIDING SPOT, CONSIDERING THE ASSETS THE NORTH KOREANS HAVE DEPLOYED OVER THE PAST 15 HOURS TO GET THEIR HANDS ON HIM!

WE'VE ASKED HIM NOT TO TRANSMIT ANYMORE UNTIL REQUESTED, SO WE CAN LOCATE HIM PRECISELY AT THE MOMENT WE DEEM SUITABLE FOR HIS EXTRACTION.

AFTER THIS BRIEFING, YOU WILL TAKE OFF TO GET INTO POSITION AT KOREAN POST 36, IN THE NO-FLY ZONE, WHERE YOU WILL REMAIN ON ALERT. WHEN THE RC-135(*) JUDGES THAT THE TIME IS RIGHT, IT'LL SEND YOU THE GREEN LIGHT FOR THE RESCUE OPERATION.

(*) See below.

WHEN THAT TIME COMES—THAT IS TO SAY, IF YOUR MISSION CAN BE COMPLETED WITH ZERO, OR CLOSE TO ZERO, RISKS OF ARMED CONFLICT, THE RC-135 WILL PROVIDE YOU WITH OUR PILOT'S LOCATION...

HE WILL BE AT MOST 10 MINUTES AWAY. YOU WILL FLY THERE NAP OF THE EARTH AND FULL SPEED. THE RC-135 WILL JAM ALL RADIO TRANSMISSIONS IN THE AREA TO PREVENT THE NORTH KOREAN TROOPS FROM ORGANISING.

TRY TO COMPLETE THIS EXTRACTION AS DISCREETLY AS POSSIBLE. ONLY USE YOUR WEAPONS IF YOU ARE UNDER DIRECT THREAT AND NEED THEM TO DISENGAGE. GOOD LUCK, GENTLEMEN!

RC-135

A recon and electronic surveillance aircraft, this four-engine plane is one of the many military versions of the venerable Boeing 707 airliner. Bristling with sensors, radars and cameras, equipped with decoders and jammers, it can follow the evolution of a ground battle by synthesising the movements of vehicles (detected by radars) and through the interception of enemy communications. With the ability to refuel in flight, it is capable of accomplishing missions of 20 hours or so. Its crew comprises 2 pilots, 2 navigators and from 15 to 20 operators.

IT'S 13:30 IN PARIS WHEN BUCK AND HIS WINGMEN TAKE OFF FOR THEIR FLIGHT DEMONSTRATION...

WHILE IN KOREA, NEAR THE SOUTHERN EDGE OF THE DMZ...

SQUINTER, FLEA JUMP, TWO MINUTES SOUTH, OVER!

THIS IS SQUINTER... DZ(1) IS CLEAR, FOX ECHO(2): 27-POINT-2, WIND FROM 260, 6 KNOTS...

NS13A

(1) Helicopter's landing (drop) zone
(2) Atmospheric pressure

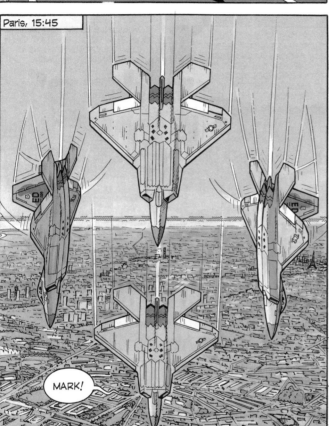

Paris, 15:45

MARK!

AND NOW WE HEAD FOR DIJON, THE FIRST WAYPOINT ON OUR TRIP. REGROUP ON ME!

NS13B

AT 16:15, AS PLANNED, THE FOUR F-22S ARE OVER THE ADRIATIC AND START THEIR REFUELLING BEHIND A KC-135 FROM NEARBY ITALY...

THEN THEY RESUME THEIR JOURNEY...

WE'RE GOING INTO SUPERCRUISE UNTIL THE ISLAND OF CORFU. WE'LL BE THERE IN HALF AN HOUR.

NS13C

MEANWHILE, IN KOREA...

WHAT ARE WE WAITING FOR?...

THE ORDER FROM THE RC-135... THERE MUST BE A PROBLEM!

FLEA JUMP, THIS IS WATCH DOG, DO YOU READ?

THIS IS FLEA JUMP... I READ YOU 5, WATCH DOG... OVER...

OPERATION BLOCKED SKIMMER IS PUSHED BACK. THE AREA IS CRAWLING WITH VEHICLES AND HELICOPTERS. WE'LL CONTACT YOU AGAIN IN TWO HOURS...

NS14A

TWO HOURS LATER...

THE SUEZ CANAL!

SIGHTSEEING IS ALL VERY NICE, BUT I'M GOING TO LODGE A COMPLAINT WITH MR MACDONNELL-DOUGLAS(*) SO HE'LL MAKE HIS SEATS SOFTER! MY BEHIND HURTS!

(*) Company that manufactures the Aces II ejector seat equipping the F-22

WHILE, NEAR THE KOREAN BORDER...

FLEA JUMP, THIS IS WATCH DOG. THE SITUATION HAS STABILISED... THE SEARCH TROOPS ARE PROBABLY MAKING CAMP FOR THE NIGHT. THE AREA IS TOO CROWDED TO THINK ABOUT AN INTERVENTION AT THE MOMENT...

... WE'LL KEEP SCANNING THE ZONE. UNLESS THE SITUATION CHANGES, WE'LL HAVE TO CANCEL THE OPERATION. NEXT CONTACT IN TWO HOURS!...

NS14B

IT'S ALMOST 21:00 LOCAL TIME WHEN BUCK'S F-22 BREAKS FORMATION OVER THE RYAD MILITARY BASE...

AT LAST! NOW WE'RE GOING TO EARN A GOOD NIGHT'S SLEEP!

SHORTLY AFTERWARDS...

WELCOME TO ARABIA!... I'M COLONEL LE VECK AND THIS IS MAJOR AL WARI OF THE ROYAL SAUDI AIR FORCE. WE'RE IN CHARGE OF ALL THE DETAILS OF YOUR STOPOVER HERE...

STOPOVER?!

OF COURSE! DIDN'T YOU KNOW?

NS14C

WHAT THE HECK! I WAS RIGHT TO THINK THIS WASN'T GOING TO BE ANY PICNIC!

FOR THE MOMENT, I'LL LEAVE YOU IN MAJOR AL WARI'S HANDS—HE'LL TAKE CARE OF FEEDING AND LODGING YOU.

ONCE YOU'RE FED AND REFRESHED, WE'LL MEET AGAIN AND I'LL GIVE YOU YOUR MISSION ORDERS AND DETAILS OF YOUR NEXT NAVIGATION.

AT THE SAME MOMENT IN KOREA...

FLEA JUMP, WATCH DOG: WE'RE CANCELLING THE OPERATION. GO BACK TO BASE. WE'LL TRY AGAIN TOMORROW NIGHT IF OUR MAN HASN'T BEEN CAPTURED BY THEN!

RYAD, 22:30, IN A ROOM INSIDE A DESERTED BUILDING...

GENTLEMEN, THE TIME HAS COME TO GIVE YOU YOUR DESTINATION...

OKINAWA, JAPAN!

HOW MANY STOPS?

NONE. 6,300 MILES IN A SINGLE LEG WITH THREE IN-FLIGHT REFUELLINGS... APPROXIMATELY EIGHT AND A HALF HOURS OF FLIGHT...

GOSH!... MY POOR BEHIND!...

NS15A

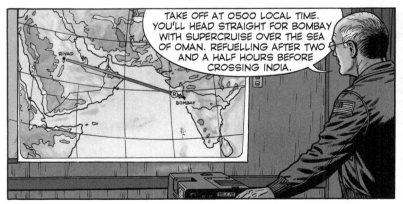

TAKE OFF AT 0500 LOCAL TIME. YOU'LL HEAD STRAIGHT FOR BOMBAY WITH SUPERCRUISE OVER THE SEA OF OMAN. REFUELLING AFTER TWO AND A HALF HOURS BEFORE CROSSING INDIA.

THE GULF OF BENGAL IN SUPERCRUISE... SECOND REFUELLING AFTER FIVE HOURS OF FLIGHT.

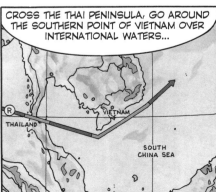

CROSS THE THAI PENINSULA, GO AROUND THE SOUTHERN POINT OF VIETNAM OVER INTERNATIONAL WATERS...

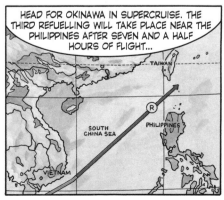

HEAD FOR OKINAWA IN SUPERCRUISE. THE THIRD REFUELLING WILL TAKE PLACE NEAR THE PHILIPPINES AFTER SEVEN AND A HALF HOURS OF FLIGHT...

... AND ONE LAST LEG ON SUPERCRUISE WILL GET YOU TO KADENA BASE AROUND 1930 LOCAL TIME.

Francis Bergèse

NS15B

WE HAVE OBTAINED ALL THE FLYOVER AUTHOR- IZATIONS FROM THE INTERESTED COUNTRIES, ON THE CONDITION THAT WE RESPECT THE FLIGHT PLAN: TIMINGS, HEADINGS, SPEEDS AND ALTITUDES...

IN CASE OF PROBLEMS, IT'S OUT OF THE QUESTION TO LAND ANYWHERE OTHER THAN AN ALLIED COUNTRY'S BASE. THE ONLY AVAILABLE ONES NEAR YOUR FLIGHT PATH ARE IN THAILAND, THE PHILIPPINES AND TAIWAN...

OTHERWISE YOU'LL HAVE TO EJECT. THE TECHNOLOGY IN THESE PLANES IS STILL MOSTLY SECRET. BETTER TO LOSE ONE THAN RISK SEEING IT CONFISCATED BY SOME UNFRIENDLY AUTHORITIES...

COULD WE KNOW WHAT WE'RE BEING SENT OVER THERE FOR?

SORRY... I HAVE NO INFORMATION ON THAT SUBJECT.

HERE ARE YOUR MISSION ORDERS, FLIGHT PLANS AND NAVIGATION SOFTWARE. A MECHANICS TEAM WILL BE THERE TO HELP YOU START UP THE PLANES. I'LL BE THERE AS WELL.

YOU HAVE FIVE HOURS LEFT TO GET SOME REST. I WON'T KEEP YOU ANY LONGER... SLEEP TIGHT!

OVER EIGHT HOURS MORE TO SPEND ON THAT BLASTED SEAT! WILL THEY HAVE SOME STRETCHERS HANDY WHEN WE LAND?

MEANWHILE, ON THE YELLOW SEA, OFF KUNSAN...

WELL, TALK ABOUT THE CATCH OF THE DAY!

?! WHAT IS IT, YONG?

WE'VE GOT A CORPSE IN THE NET!

I'LL CALL PORT AUTHORITIES!

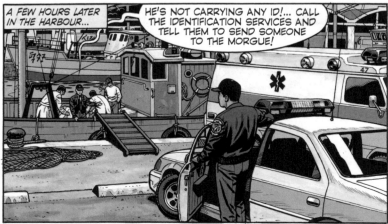

A FEW HOURS LATER IN THE HARBOUR...

HE'S NOT CARRYING ANY ID!... CALL THE IDENTIFICATION SERVICES AND TELL THEM TO SEND SOMEONE TO THE MORGUE!

WHILE 6 MILES FROM THERE, ON THE AIRBASE...

HAS ANYBODY SEEN CHUNG? THEY'RE LOOKING ALL OVER FOR HIM AT THE WING'S(*) SECRETARIAT!...

(*) Unit

NS16B

YOU CAN LOOK FOR HIM! HE DIDN'T COME TO WORK THIS MORNING... HIS WIFE'S LOOKING FOR HIM TOO... SHE CALLED: HE LEFT YESTERDAY MORNING AND HASN'T BEEN BACK SINCE!

GOOD LORD!

WHAT'S UP WITH YOU?

I'M THINKING OF SOMETHING... MAYBE IT'S SILLY... BUT... WHEN I LEFT SATURDAY NIGHT, HE STAYED ALONE WITH MAX, WHO WAS PREPARING HIS FLIGHT FOR THE NEXT DAY...

SO?

SO I'M THINKING HE COULD VERY WELL HAVE HAD SOMETHING TO DO WITH THE PROBLEMS IN MAX'S NAVIGATION SYSTEM!...

YOU READ TOO MANY SPY NOVELS!

HOW DO YOU EXPLAIN THAT FROM THE MOMENT MAX WAS BLINDED AND TRIED TO CHANGE HIS WAYPOINT, HIS AUTOPILOT KEPT TAKING HIM STRAIGHT TO NORTH KOREA REGARDLESS OF WHICH NUMBER HE SELECTED?!

WITHOUT BEING ABLE TO SEE ANYTHING, HE COULD HAVE HIT THE WRONG SWITCH...

NO! NO!... NOT "BLOODY" MAXWELL, PAL, NOT HIM!

NS17A

THEN MAYBE A MALFUNCTION OF THE ONBOARD COMPUTER... IT'S ALWAYS POSSIBLE!

IF CHUNG WAS HERE, I'D SAY YES... BUT I CAN'T HELP MAKING A CONNECTION BETWEEN HIS DISAPPEARANCE AND MAX'S PROBLEMS. I THINK THAT WE SHOULD CALL THE POLICE, ISSUE AN APB!

TALK TO THE COLONEL!

I'M GOING THERE RIGHT NOW!

AT THE SAME TIME IN RYAD...

WHERE ARE THEY GOING?

IT'S TOP SECRET, MAJOR... SORRY!... BUT THE TRIP WILL BE LONG!

SEVERAL HOURS LATER, EARLY AFTERNOON AT THE KUNSAN MORGUE...

영안실

IT WAS HIM... 하느님 맙소사!(*)

(*) God help us!

MY CONDOLENCES, MRS CHUNG...

NS17B

19

WHAT HAPPENED TO HIM?

THE JOINT ENQUIRY FROM THE POLICE AND THE US AIR FORCE WILL CERTAINLY DETERMINE THAT... BE STRONG!

MEANWHILE...

WE'RE PASSING BOMBAY!... EIGHT OKTAS CLOUD COVER... SO MUCH FOR SIGHTSEEING!

2 HOURS 50 MINUTES SINCE WE TOOK OFF... IT FEELS LIKE FOREVER TO ME!

HANG ON TIGHT, FROGGY!... ONLY FIVE MORE HOURS PLUS CHANGE!

WITH TWO REFUELLINGS TO PASS THE TIME!

CAPT FROGGY TUCKSON

TWO HOURS AND 15 MINUTES LATER...

WE'VE DONE OVER HALF THE TRIP. IN 15 MINUTES WE'LL BE OVER THAILAND!

NS18A

AT THE SAME TIME IN OKINAWA...

SCOTT, DO YOU THINK THAT AFTER SUCH A TRIP THESE MEN WILL BE FIT TO LEAVE FOR KOREA IMMEDIATELY?

TWO OF THEM SERVED UNDER ME DURING A SPECIAL OPERATION IN BOSNIA(*): DANNY AND TUCKSON... THEY'RE TOUGH CUSTOMERS! WE CAN COUNT ON THEM.

(*) See Ghost Squadron.

VERY WELL... THIS IS THE CONFERENCE ROOM WHERE MY BEST TACTICAL OFFICERS ARE DRAWING UP EVERY ELEMENT OF OPERATION "SNEAKY SERPENT." FROM NOW ON, THEY'RE AT YOUR DISPOSAL.

CONFERENCE ROOM

REST ROOM LAVAT

OVER THE SOUTH CHINA SEA, AS THE DAY DRAWS TO A CLOSE, THE F-22S ARE SPEEDING ON THEIR WAY TOWARDS JAPAN AT 1000 MILES PER HOUR...

GOSH! WE'VE BEEN FLYING FOR 7 HOURS AND 20 MINUTES, AND MY GPS(*) IS SAYING IT'S ALREADY 1720!... I'VE JUST LOST FIVE HOURS OF MY PRECIOUS LIFE!

THAT'S THE INCONVENIENCE OF FLYING UP THE TIME ZONES! WHEN WE ARRIVE, YOU'LL BE MISSING ANOTHER ONE. QUITE A SHORT DAY!

(*) Global Positioning System. This device, which constantly measures geographical location, also gives the local time.

NS18B

LIGHTNING LEADER HERE: I MADE CONTACT WITH THE THIRD TANKER... FIVE MINUTES AHEAD. START REDUCING SPEED.

TWENTY MINUTES LATER, THE FOUR "RAPTORS" HAVE TOPPED OFF THEIR TANKS AND ARE LEAVING THE KC-135 BEHIND.

THANKS FOR THE NICE BOTTLE, NANNY! SAFE TRIP HOME!

WE'RE ALMOST THERE, KIDS... ONLY ONE HOUR AND 45 MINUTES OF FLIGHT LEFT!

MEANWHILE, IN KADENA...

WELL, I THINK WE WORKED EVERYTHING OUT, SIR...

ALL THE HELICOPTERS FOR THE OPERATION, US AIR FORCE AND US ARMY, SHOULD BE ASSEMBLED IN OSAN SHORTLY. ALL WE'RE MISSING ARE THE F-22S...

THEY'LL BE HERE IN ABOUT AN HOUR. I'LL TAKE CARE OF THEIR ARRIVAL.

COLONEL CAMPBELL, COLONEL FISCHER, YOU'RE TAKING OFF FOR OSAN IMMEDIATELY AND WILL TAKE CARE OF BRIEFING THE HELICOPTER CREWS AND SELECTED PERSONNEL.

CAN WE CONSIDER THE TIMING AS SET IN STONE, SIR?

NS19A

THAT'S AFFIRMATIVE. THE ONLY POSSIBLE REASON THAT I—AND ONLY I—WOULD COUNTERMAND THOSE ORDERS IS IF THE RC-135 DETECTED A LARGE INCREASE OF NORTH KOREAN TROOPS AROUND THE LOCATION OF OUR INTERVENTION. BUT I DON'T THINK WE HAVE TO WORRY ABOUT THAT... THINGS ARE STABLE ON THAT FRONT.

AN HOUR LATER, THE F-22S ARRIVE DISCREETLY AT KADENA AIRBASE WITH A LONG APPROACH OVER THE SEA...

... FOLLOWED BY A SHORT LANDING AT THE VERY BEGINNING OF THE LONGEST RUNWAY...

... AND TAXIING BY WAY OF PERIPHERAL ROADS TOWARDS A PARKING AREA IN THE MOST SECRET PART OF THE BASE...

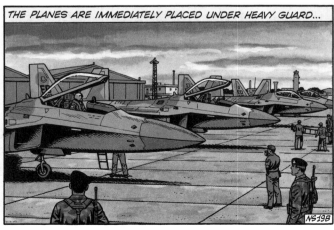

THE PLANES ARE IMMEDIATELY PLACED UNDER HEAVY GUARD...

NS19B

SOON...

WELCOME TO OKINAWA, BOYS!

WHAT?!... OH, NO!

?

WHAT'S WRONG WITH YOU, FROGGY?

GEN... GENERAL X(*)!... MY WORST FEAR IS COMING TRUE!

(*) See Ghost Squadron.

I'M GENERAL SCOTT! NICE TO SEE YOU AGAIN, DANNY AND TUCKSON... GLAD TO MEET YOU, TUMBLER AND JACKSON! IF YOU'D CARE TO CLIMB ABOARD?...

FIRST OF ALL, I IMAGINE YOU NEED A NICE SHOWER AND A GOOD MEAL!...

I'LL TAKE A LONG SOAK FOR MY HINDQUARTERS!

DON'T PAY ATTENTION TO HIM, SIR... OUR FRIEND FROGGY HAS BEEN A BIT GRUMPY SINCE YESTERDAY MORNING!

NS20A

MEANWHILE, IN OSAN...

GENTLEMEN... AN EXCESSIVE CONCENTRATION OF NORTH KOREAN TROOPS PREVENTED US FROM EXTRACTING OUR PILOT LAST NIGHT...

THOSE TROOPS HAVE DISPERSED AND WE'LL BE ABLE TO TRY AGAIN TONIGHT. NO CHANGES... YOU WILL WAIT AT KOREAN POST M-36 AND STAY ON ALERT THERE FROM MIDNIGHT ON. THEY WILL RELAY THE ORDER TO GO. ANY QUESTIONS?

COULDN'T SUCH DISPERSAL BE A SIGN THAT OUR PILOT MIGHT HAVE BEEN CAPTURED, SIR?

I DID SAY DISPERSAL AND NOT DEPARTURE. OUR PILOT HAS TURNED ON HIS BEACON SEVERAL TIMES AT THE REQUEST OF THE RC-135, WHICH ALLOWED US TO CONFIRM HE WAS STILL IN THE SAME SPOT...

ARE WE CERTAIN IT'S NOT THE NORTH KOREANS USING THE BEACON TO LURE US INTO A TRAP AND SHOOT DOWN OUR CHOPPERS?

WE CANNOT BE CERTAIN, BUT IF THERE WAS A TRAP, OUR RC-135 WOULD BE ABLE TO DETECT ITS PREPARATIONS...

OTHERWISE, THEIR ASSETS WOULD BE INSUFFICIENT TO POSE A REAL THREAT...

Francis Bergèse

NS20B

IN KADENA, BUCK AND HIS FRIENDS ARE GETTING SETTLED IN THE ROOMS THAT HAVE BEEN ASSIGNED TO THEM...

!... THOSE RASCALS!

THE BASTARDS!

THEY'LL PAY FOR THAT!

AN HOUR LATER, REFRESHED AND WEARING CLEAN CLOTHES, THE FOUR PILOTS ARE FINISHING A WELL-DESERVED MEAL WHEN...

GEE! IT'S AWFULLY GOOD WHEN YOU'RE HUNGRY!

GOOD, BUT SMALL PORTIONS!

PLEASE?

IF YOU'RE FINISHED, GENERAL SCOTT IS WAITING FOR YOU IN THE CONFERENCE ROOM. I WILL TAKE YOU THERE.

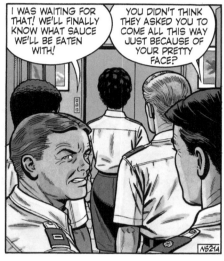
I WAS WAITING FOR THAT! WE'LL FINALLY KNOW WHAT SAUCE WE'LL BE EATEN WITH!

YOU DIDN'T THINK THEY ASKED YOU TO COME ALL THIS WAY JUST BECAUSE OF YOUR PRETTY FACE?

SPEAKING OF WHICH, CORPORAL, YOU KNOW YOU'RE QUITE GIFTED IN THAT DEPARTMENT TOO?

HE RECOVERS QUICKLY, DOESN'T HE? I'VE ALWAYS BEEN QUITE IMPRESSED BY THAT!

IF YOU HAVE A MOMENT TOMORROW, I CAN GIVE YOU THE ADDRESS OF A PLACE IN PARIS WHERE THEY SERVE THE BEST SNAILS...

HERE WE ARE. GO IN!

TAKE YOUR SEATS, FOLKS!... YOU'RE FINALLY GOING TO LEARN THE REASON FOR THIS LONG TRIP!

I FEAR THE WORST!

FIRST THE SITUATION: YOU MUST HAVE HEARD THAT ONE OF OUR F-16S WAS SHOT DOWN IN NORTH KOREA AS A RESULT OF A CONSPIRACY WE HAVEN'T BEEN ABLE TO PROVE YET. THE DATA FROM THE EARLY INQUIRY ARE IN THE FOLDERS IN FRONT OF YOU.

THE PYONGYANG(*) GOVERNMENT IS USING THIS INCIDENT FOR PROPAGANDA AND HAS INVITED JOURNALISTS FROM ALL OVER THE WORLD TO A PRESS CONFERENCE TOMORROW AT THE CRASH SITE ITSELF...

(*) Capital of North Korea

WE ARE CERTAIN THAT THIS CRASH IS THE CULMINATION OF AN OPERATION CAREFULLY PREPARED BY THE NORTH KOREAN INTELLIGENCE AGENCY. THEREFORE, OUR GOVERNMENT HAS DECIDED TO CAUSE THIS MEDIA MANIPULATION TO FAIL, BY USING ANY MEANS NECESSARY...

WELL, THEN, IT CAN'T BE OF ANY CONCERN TO US. WHY ARE YOU TELLING US ALL THIS WHEN WE'RE DREAMING OF A SOFT BED?!

WE'RE GOING TO SEND A GREAT NUMBER OF HELICOPTERS TO THE SITE TO RECOVER THE WRECKAGE AND CLEAN UP THE AREA. YOUR JOB WILL BE TO CREATE A DIVERSION IN THE MEANTIME BY KEEPING THE ENEMY'S RADARS AND FIGHTERS OCCUPIED...

WHAT?

WE'D RISK GIFTING THE COMMIES WITH A CRASHED F-22 INSTEAD OF AN F-16?!

SONNY! LET GENERAL SCOTT FINISH! THEN YOU CAN INTERVENE!...

IN FACT, THE OPERATION ITSELF SHOULD TAKE PLACE IN LESS THAN AN HOUR. THROUGH SOUTH KOREAN INTELLIGENCE, WE KNOW THAT THE SITE IS ONLY GUARDED BY A HANDFUL OF MEN...

... A COMPANY AT THE MOST... OUR SPECIAL FORCES, ARRIVING FIRST, WILL QUICKLY BE ABLE TO SECURE THE ZONE. IT WON'T BE ANYTHING MORE SERIOUS THAN THE LAND, AIR AND SEA SKIRMISHES THAT TAKE PLACE EVERY YEAR BETWEEN THE TWO KOREAS...

BUT WE MUST PREVENT THE ENEMY'S FAST ASSETS—HELICOPTERS AND FIGHTERS—FROM INTERVENING WHILE THE AIR FORCE SPECIALISTS CLEAN UP THE GROUND.

ANY EXCESSIVE FORCE COULD ESCALATE THE SITUATION, EVEN ALL THE WAY UP TO ANOTHER KOREAN WAR... AND THAT'S WHERE YOU COME IN...

NS22A

FIRST, BY DRIVING THE AREA'S RADAR COVERAGE INSANE, EACH OF YOU IN A DIFFERENT SECTOR SURROUNDING THE MISSION OBJECTIVE, BY CANCELLING THE STEALTH ASPECT OF YOUR PLANES, EITHER BY OPENING THE WEAPONS BAYS OR BY TURNING ON YOUR OWN RADARS...

IF ANY HELICOPTERS ATTEMPT TO BRING REINFORCEMENTS, YOU WILL PRETEND TO GO AFTER THEM BY TURNING ON YOUR RADARS AND, IF NECESSARY, BY FIRING YOUR GUNS ACROSS THEIR NOSES TO GET THEM TO CHANGE DIRECTION...

THIS IS THE BROAD OUTLINE OF YOUR MISSION; YOU'LL FIND A MORE DETAILED PLAN IN THE FILES YOU WERE GIVEN...

FILES THAT WE WILL DESTROY AS SOON AS YOU'VE READ THEM.

WHY NOT USE F-117S(*)?

THE F-117 IS TOO SLOW AND INSUFFICIENTLY MANOEUVRABLE TO ESCAPE A MIG FIGHTER SAFELY. WHEREAS, WITH THE POWER AND AGILITY OF THE F-22, IT WILL BE CHILD'S PLAY FOR YOU TO TRICK THEM WITHOUT RISK!

(*) Stealth fighter-bomber that entered service in the US Air Force in 1988

WITHOUT RISK!... EASY FOR YOU TO SAY!... WE'RE NOT TOO SCARED OF MISSILES, BUT A GOOD BURST OF 30MM SHELLS FROM A NORTH KOREAN FIGHTER ACE, AND WE CAN KISS OUR STEALTH GOODBYE... IF IT DOESN'T SEND US STRAIGHT INTO THE GROUND!

IT WILL ALL TAKE PLACE CLOSE TO THE BORDER... IF ANYTHING GOES WRONG, YOU CAN BE IN SOUTH KOREA IN NO TIME AND UNDER OUR OWN FIGHTER COVER!

NS22B

A MECHANICS TEAM SPECIALIZED IN THE F-22 CAME FROM YOUR BASE AT EDWARDS(*) AND IS CHECKING YOUR PLANES AND LOADING THE GUNS.

YOU'LL TAKE OFF AT 2330. IN ONE HOUR OF SUPERCRUISE, YOU'LL REACH THE ISLAND OF INCHON. THEN YOU'LL HEAD NORTHEAST TO THE NO-FLY ZONE AT THE LEVEL OF YOUR MISSION AREA. THE RC-135 WILL GIVE YOU THE SIGNAL FOR THE START OF THE OPERATION.

(*) USAF test centre in the Mojave Desert, California

AN AWACS(*) WILL PROVIDE AERIAL SURVEILLANCE AND WILL WARN YOU OF ALL AIR MOVEMENTS TOWARDS YOUR RESPECTIVE SECTORS.

(*) Airborne Warning and Control System: a 707 Boeing converted into a flying radar

ONCE IT'S ALL OVER, YOU'LL HEAD BACK TO INCHON AND THE YELLOW SEA, WHERE A KC-135 WILL ALLOW YOU TO REFUEL. A BIT OF SUPER-CRUISE, AND AROUND 0245 YOU'LL BE BACK HERE, WHERE YOUR BEDS WILL BE READY TO WELCOME YOU!

WHY NOT LAND IN KOREA?... WE COULD BE IN BED AN HOUR EARLIER!...

WE WOULD PREFER THAT THE F-22S WERE ONLY SEEN HERE... THIS BASE BEING ON AN ISLAND, IT IS MUCH LESS EXPOSED TO ACCIDENTAL SIGHTSEEING.

NONETHELESS, IN CASE OF TROUBLE, YOU CAN LAND IN KOREA... BUT PREFERABLY ON ONE OF THE TWO US AIR FORCE BASES: OSAN OR KUNSAN.

ONE QUESTION, SIR... AS FAR AS I KNOW, THE PILOT OF THAT F-16 WAS CAPTURED... SO WHY BOTHER...?

LIES! DISINFORMATION! PROPAGANDA!... AN EXTRACTION MISSION FAILED LAST NIGHT, BUT WE'RE TRYING AGAIN TONIGHT USING THE DIVERSION YOU'LL CREATE, AND WE'RE CONFIDENT WE CAN BRING HIM BACK!

NS23A

FORTY MINUTES AFTER MID-NIGHT, SURVEILLANCE POST MC-78, ALONG THE DMZ...

LISTEN!

THEY'RE COMING!

TCHOWTCHOWTCHOWTCHOW

THERE'RE TWO!

OUR NEXT WAYPOINT IS TWO MILES BEYOND THE DMZ... THAT WAY, THE ENEMY OBSERVATION POSTS LOCATED NEAR IT, ALONG OUR PATH, WILL HAVE REPORTED US ON A DUE NORTH HEADING...

WHEREAS WE'LL HAVE TURNED 60 DEGREES TO THE WEST!

HOPEFULLY OUR GUY IS STILL THERE... HE MUST BE GETTING TIRED OF WAITING!

THIS TIME SHOULD BE THE ONE: WHEN WE TOOK OFF, WE WERE TOLD THAT THE NORTH KOREAN TROOPS HAD LEFT THE SECTOR!

NS23B

WOW! DO YOU KNOW HOW MANY THERE ARE, SERGEANT?

A DOZEN! THEY'RE ON TIME!... WE SHOULD SEE AS MANY AGAIN PASS US IN EIGHT MINUTES.

WHAT THE KOREAN GUARDS NEITHER SEE NOR HEAR ARE THE FOUR STEALTH AIRCRAFT FLYING BARELY A HUNDRED FEET ABOVE IN A QUIET WHISPER OF ENGINES ON LOW THRUST...

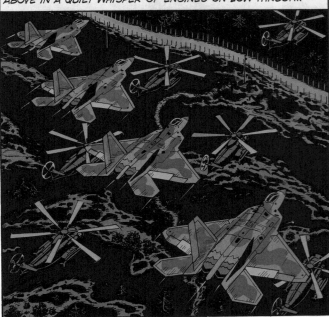

THEY'RE CROSSING INTO THE DMZ... EVERYTHING'S OK!

PERFECT TIMING!... IN ONE MINUTE THEY'LL FLY OVER THE NORTH KOREAN LINES.

LET'S HOPE THE ELEMENT OF SURPRISE WILL WORK...

AND NOW WE'RE IN THE MIDDLE OF NO MAN'S LAND. A CIRCLE OF 10 DEGREES PER SECOND WILL LET THE HELICOPTERS GAIN ENOUGH OF A HEAD-START...

... THAT WE'LL BE RIGHT ABOVE THEM WHEN THEY CROSS THE NORTH KOREAN LINES...

SOON... THE TWO "PAVE LOW" HAVE CROSSED OVER... THERE'S A LITTLE AUTOMATIC WEAPONS FIRE, BUT NOTHING TOO HEAVY FOR THE MOMENT...

THERE WE ARE... THEIR FIRE IS INTENSIFYING, BUT IT'S STILL LIGHT WEAPONS...

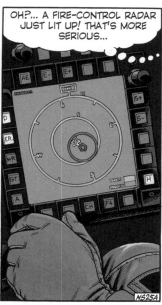

OH?... A FIRE-CONTROL RADAR JUST LIT UP! THAT'S MORE SERIOUS...

NS25A

SUDDENLY THE SKY IS LIT BY LARGE-CALIBRE TRACER ROUNDS...

RATTLESNAKE 1 TO THOSE BIRDS MOST EXPOSED TO THE FIRE: SWITCH ON YOUR ECMS(1)! DROP CHAFF(2)!

(1) Electronic Counter-Measures
(2) Cloud of metallic fibres designed to jam radars

ONE OF THE CHOPPERS GOT HIT... IT'S TURNING BACK...

SHORTLY AFTERWARDS, AFTER GETTING PAST THE DEFENSIVE LINES...

IT'S SETTLING DOWN... OUR TURN NOW!

NS25B

EACH TO HIS OWN SECTOR... WE'RE GOING TO START TICKLING THEIR RADARS!...

Francis Bergese

NS25C

PYTHON 2, PYTHON 2, THIS IS OWLEYE!... AIR ACTIVITY IN YOUR SECTOR: TWO PLANES JUST TOOK OFF FROM WONSAN AIRBASE AND ARE HEADING TOWARDS RATTLESNAKE PATH...

WE'RE SENDING YOU THE REAL-TIME TELEMETRY. TRY TO LURE THESE AIRCRAFT TOWARDS THE NORTHEAST!

WITHOUT HAVING TO TURN ON HIS RADAR, TUMBLER SEES ALL THE DATA RELATING TO THE THREAT APPEAR ON ONE OF HIS CRT SCREENS...

OKAY... I'LL CROSS THEIR PATH IN FOUR MINUTES... IT'S PLAY TIME!

FLEA JUMP, WATCH DOG... WE GOT IN TOUCH WITH YOUR MAN...

COORDINATES: N382958, E1268204. HEADING ADJUSTMENT MINUS SEVEN DEGREES... YOU'LL BE THERE IN FOUR MINUTES.

ALTITUDE 15,000 FEET... HEADING NORTHWEST... IT'S TIME TO MAKE MYSELF KNOWN!

OPENING THE DOORS OF HIS INTERNAL BAY, BUCK CAUSES A SERIOUS DEGRADATION OF HIS AIRCRAFT'S STEALTH PROFILE FOR A FEW DOZEN SECONDS...

LITTLE BY LITTLE, A SERIES OF SPOTS APPEARS ON HIS THREAT RECOGNITION SCREEN...

THE CENTRAL LONG-RANGE RADARS HAVE JUST ALERTED LOCAL AIR DEFENCE... BETTER NOT HANG AROUND HERE!

BAY DOORS CLOSED AND CHECKED... CHANGING VECTOR AND ALTITUDE...

AND HERE COME THE SAMS(*)!

(*) Surface-to-Air Missiles

AS THE GUIDANCE RADARS LOSE CONTACT WITH THEIR TARGET, THE MISSILES KEEP CLIMBING UNTIL THEIR ENGINES DIE; THEIR CONTROLLERS HAVE NO CHOICE THEN BUT TO TRIGGER THE SELF-DESTRUCT SYSTEM.

EACH IN HIS OWN SECTOR, BUCK'S WINGMEN HAVE PROCEEDED IN SIMILAR FASHION, TRIGGERING RADAR ALERT AFTER RADAR ALERT...

THOSE POOR RADAR OPERATORS MUST BE WONDERING IF THEIR OLD RUSSIAN EQUIPMENT ISN'T CROAKING ON THEM!

FOR TUMBLER, THOUGH, THE SITUATION IS A BIT MORE DELICATE BECAUSE OF THE TWO NORTH KOREAN FIGHTERS HE IS SUPPOSED TO LEAD AWAY...

THERE THEY ARE... THEY'RE TURNING TOWARDS THE SPOT WHERE I CLOSED MY BAY DOORS...

MIG-21S...

PYTHON 2, THIS IS OWLEYE... FOUR MORE FIGHTERS JUST TOOK OFF FROM WONSAN AND ARE HEADING YOUR WAY!

TIME TO BLOW THIS JOINT... I'M DIVING AND HEADING AWAY FROM HERE...

WATCH DOG, FLEA JUMP. THIRTY SECONDS FROM TARGET!

HURRY UP, FLEA JUMP!... TWO HELICOPTERS ARE LEAVING A CAMP TWO MILES AWAY AND ARE HEADING TOWARDS YOU... BEARING 240!

WATCH DOG, FLEA JUMP, WE'RE OVER THE TARGET. IT'S A SMALL COUNTRY BRIDGE OVER A CANAL. CAN'T SEE ANYONE!

WE'RE BEING SHOT AT! THERE ARE STILL SOLDIERS IN THE AREA!

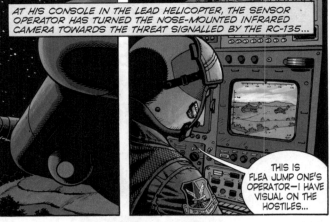

AT HIS CONSOLE IN THE LEAD HELICOPTER, THE SENSOR OPERATOR HAS TURNED THE NOSE-MOUNTED INFRARED CAMERA TOWARDS THE THREAT SIGNALLED BY THE RC-135...

THIS IS FLEA JUMP ONE'S OPERATOR—I HAVE VISUAL ON THE HOSTILES...

... THEY'RE HINDS!(*)

FLEA JUMP ONE AND TWO, FALL BACK TO WAYPOINT 4 NOW... WE'LL WARN THE SOUTH KOREAN POST IN YOUR PATH.

(*) Russian-made combat helicopter

THE AREA IS OCCUPIED BY INFANTRY!... OUR MAN MUST HAVE BEEN CAPTURED!

GET BACK TO BASE FOR DEBRIEFING, FLEA JUMP. YOU'LL FIGURE THINGS OUT WITH THE BOSS.

COPY THAT WATCH DOG, COMING HOME.

MEANWHILE, SOME 1.2 MILES TO THE NORTHEAST...

SILENCE THE HEAVY WEAPONS FIRST!

REAR GUNNER, COPY!

LEFT GUNNER, COPY!

GO! GO! GO! I WANT ALL REMAINING POCKETS OF RESISTANCE SUPPRESSED QUICKLY! YOU HAVE SIX MINUTES BEFORE THE AIR FORCE ENGINEERS GET HERE!

AT THAT INSTANT, 20 MILES TO THE SOUTHEAST...

THERE'S THE SECOND WAVE... THERE'S GOING TO BE SOME FIREWORKS ON THE OTHER SIDE!

THESE HAVE A DIFFERENT HEADING... THEY WON'T CROSS AT THE SAME SPOT!...

MAN! WHEN THE AMERICANS WANT TO GET A PILOT BACK, THEY DON'T GO FOR HALF-MEASURES!

MEANWHILE, HIGH IN THE SKY OVER THE YELLOW SEA...

PYTHON ONE, THIS IS OWLEYE... ALERT! FOUR JETS JUST TOOK OFF FROM OKSAN-NI AIRBASE AND ARE HEADING TOWARDS YOUR SECTOR... THE LEADER TURNED HIS RADAR ON. YOU SHOULD BE ABLE TO SEE IT!

NS.29A

I DID SEE HIM... BUT I HAD NO IDEA THERE WERE FOUR OF THEM!...

COL. BUCK DANNY

WARNING! ANOTHER PATROL OF FOUR TOOK OFF AFTER THE FIRST...

THIS ONE'S TAKING ANOTHER DIRECTION... PYTHON THREE, THIS NEW DELIVERY MIGHT WELL BE FOR YOU!

OK... THE LEADER HAS ALSO TURNED ON HIS RADAR!...

JUDGING BY THEIR PERFORMANCES, THEY'RE MOST LIKELY MIG-29S. KEEP THEM BUSY, BUT NO UNNECESSARY RISKS, BOYS!

MAJ DICK JACKSON

PYTHON FOUR, THIS IS OWLEYE... JOIN PYTHON TWO IN HIS SECTOR AND TRY TO DRAW SOME OF THE SIX FIGHTERS HUNTING HIM TOWARDS YOU.

I WAS NICE AND COSY, HAVING FUN DRIVING A FEW RADARS INSANE, AND NOW POOR TUMB NEEDS MY HELP!... RIGHT! LET'S GO SAMPLE SOME MIGS!

CAPT FROGGY TUCKSON

NS.29B

AT THE SAME TIME, NEAR THE F-16 WRECKAGE...

GATHER THE PRISONERS IN THE SOUTHERN HOLLOW! HAVE THEM CARRY THEIR DEAD AND WOUNDED!

THE SCRAPPERS ARE HERE! CLEAR THE AREA! CLEAR THE AREA!

GET RID OF THE PODIUM AND BENCHES! A CHOPPER CAN LAND HERE!

HOW'S IT GOING, CAPTAIN?

COULDN'T BE BETTER, SIR! WE'VE SECURED THE ZONE!... WE ONLY HAVE A FEW SPORADIC ENGAGEMENTS LEFT TO THE NORTH AND EAST!

LET'S HOPE THE CLEAN-UP WILL BE QUICK! WE'D BETTER BE DONE WITH IT BEFORE THE REINFORCEMENTS ARRIVE!

MEANWHILE, BUCK...

CLIMBING... WHILE MY FOUR HOUNDS ARE LOOKING FOR ME CLOSE TO THE GROUND!... FOR THE MOMENT, IT'S A PRETTY FUN GAME.

SAMS IN THE AIR TO THE SOUTH... DICK MUST HAVE BEEN DETECTED...

I HAVE TO GET THEIR ATTENTION TO RELIEVE THE PRESSURE ON HIM...

SEVERAL TIMES THE PILOT OPENS AND CLOSES THE DOOR OF HIS INTERNAL WEAPON BAY...

THIS IS OWLEYE. WE'VE DETECTED YOU, PYTHON ONE... DON'T OVERDO IT: THE SECOND MIG-29 PATROL IS NOW HEADING TOWARDS YOU, AND THE FIRST ONE IS PRACTICALLY BELOW YOU!

GOOD HEAVENS! DICK!

... A SAM GOT DICK!

CAUGHT UP IN HIS EMOTION, BUCK HAS FORGOTTEN HIS DELICATE SITUATION FOR A FEW SECONDS...

KRRAA

DANG IT!

A FEW TOO MANY...

YOU'LL BE SORRY YOU CAME, DIRTY IMPERIALIST LACKEY!

I GOT TAKEN LIKE A ROOKIE!

NS31A

WHAT'S GOING ON, PYTHON ONE?... WE HAVE AN ECHO OF YOU: YOU'VE LOST 30% OF YOUR STEALTH!

A GUN HIT... MY RIGHT NOZZLE HAS A PROBLEM: THE EXIT TEMPERATURE IS CLIMBING DANGEROUSLY... I'M SHUTTING OFF THE ENGINE.

ABORT IMMEDIATELY, PYTHON ONE. EMERGENCY(*) AT OSAN. WATCH DOG WILL JAM THE SEARCH RADARS IN YOUR SECTOR. APPARENTLY THE MIGS LOST YOU... THEY DON'T DARE TURN ON THEIR RADARS FOR FEAR OF BEING LOCATED BY YOU IN TURN!

(*) As in emergency landing

I SAW A SAM BLOW UP A PLANE TOWARDS PYTHON THREE... WHAT ABOUT IT?

THEY SHOT DOWN ONE OF THEIR OWN AIRCRAFT!... PYTHON THREE IS FINE—HE JUST SIGNALLED HIS PRESENCE BY OPENING HIS BAY DOORS TO ATTRACT THE MIGS THAT ARE LOOKING FOR YOU...

NS31B

TWO MINUTES LATER, AT VERY LOW ALTITUDE AND DOING 500 MPH, BUCK'S DAMAGED F-22 CROSSES THE NORTH KOREAN LINE AGAIN WITHOUT INCIDENT.

LESS THAN 15 MINUTES LATER, HE'S ON APPROACH AT OSAN.

PYTHON ONE ON FINAL, RUNWAY 26(*).

WIND FROM 245, 6 KNOTS... LAND LONG AND TAKE THE LAST TAXIWAY TO THE LEFT...

(*) Runway aligned on 260°

HE'S IMMEDIATELY LED TO A DISCREET PARKING AREA SURROUNDED BY ARMED SOLDIERS...

FOLLOW ME

OSAN 51 FW

WELCOME TO OSAN, SIR... MAJOR DODGE, IN CHARGE OF THIS IMPROMPTU WELCOME!

NS 32A

WOOOW! YOU'VE MET THE NORTH KOREANS UP CLOSE AND PERSONAL, LOOKS LIKE! WERE YOU COVERING THE "PAVE LOW"?

IN A WAY, YES...

WE'LL PUT YOU UP WITH THE "PAVE LOW" CREWS. UNFORTUNATELY, THEY CAME BACK WITHOUT COLONEL MAXWELL... WE FEAR HE MAY HAVE BEEN CAPTURED FOR REAL THIS TIME...

MAXWELL... DO YOU MEAN MAX "BLOODY" MAXWELL?

DO YOU KNOW HIM, SIR?

I WAS HIS XO BACK WHEN HE COMMANDED THE 64TH AGGRESSOR SQUADRON(*)... SO IT WAS HIM WHO EJECTED OVER THE NORTH SUNDAY MORNING?

(*) Read The Aggressors.

IT'S A STRANGE BUSINESS... HE WAS BLINDED BY AN INTENSE RED LIGHT—PROBABLY A LASER—AND HIS NAVIGATION SYSTEM TOOK HIM STRAIGHT NORTH...

TAKE ME TO THE "PAVE LOW" BOSS.

YES, SIR.

NS32B

34

MAJOR ROGERS, THIS IS COLONEL BUCK DANNY WHO'S JUST ARRIVED. HE WAS PROVIDING YOUR COVER... BUT SHHH, IT'S TOP SECRET!

GREETINGS, SIR. PARDON MY CURIOSITY: WERE YOU THERE WITH AN F-16?...

SHHH!... TOP SECRET!

F-117, EH? IT'S STILL GUTSY!... WITH ALL DUE RESPECT, SIR!

TELL ME, ROGERS... YOU'RE COMING BACK FROM THE SECTOR WHERE MAXWELL EJECTED AND YOU DIDN'T FIND HIM?

THAT'S AFFIRMATIVE, SIR... AND ALL THE MORE SURPRISING SINCE THE RC-135 WAS READING HIS BEACON A COUPLE OF MINUTES BEFORE!

AT THAT MOMENT WE WERE FLYING TOO LOW TO READ IT, BUT ONCE WE GOT TO THE SITE, IF HE'D BEEN THERE WE COULDN'T HAVE MISSED HIM!

IT COULD BE THE BEACON BROKE DOWN... DID YOU LOOK ABSOLUTELY EVERYWHERE?

WE WERE UNDER FIRE AND SOME "HINDS" WERE HEADING OUR WAY... IN SUCH CIRCUM- STANCES, YOU DON'T WAIT AROUND!

NS33A

THE COORDINATES PROVIDED BY THE RC-135 LED US TO A SMALL BRIDGE OVER A CANAL... IF MAXWELL HAD BEEN HIDDEN UNDER- NEATH, HE'D HAVE COME OUT WHEN HE HEARD US!...

ARE THERE PLANS FOR YOU GOING BACK?

WE'RE ON STAND-BY... IF IT TURNS OUT HE HASN'T BEEN CAPTURED, WE'LL UNDOUBTEDLY GO BACK.

IF THAT'S THE CASE, WILL YOU HAVE A SEAT FOR ME?... MAXWELL'S A FRIEND... I'D LIKE TO GO!

MEANWHILE... EVERYTHING'S QUIET, SIR! THE OPERATION IS GOING ACCORD- ING TO PLANS!...

THE CALM BEFORE THE STORM... LET'S MOVE IT!

PYTHON TWO AND FOUR, THIS IS OWLEYE... HERE'S SOME WORK FOR YOU: 11 HELICOP- TERS ARE HEADING TOWARDS THE TARGET SECTOR, COMING FROM THE NORTH... YOU'LL HAVE TO SLOW THEM DOWN!

NS33B

PYTHON TWO, THEY'RE 22 NAUTICAL MILES(*), BEARING 3-1-2 FROM POINT NOVEMBER-ECHO, THE CENTRE OF YOUR SECTOR.

(*) Approximately 25 miles

PYTHON FOUR: BEARING 3-4-8, 47 NAUTICAL MILES FROM POINT SIERRA-ECHO.

AS IF WE WEREN'T BUSY ENOUGH WITH THE MIGS!

PYTHON THREE, YOU'RE NOT GOING TO BE RESTING: FROM YOUR CENTRAL POINT SIERRA-WHISKY, TURN TO A 0-3-5 BEARING...

FOUR AIRCRAFT FROM PYONG-NI AIRBASE ARE JOINING THE HELICOPTERS. THEY MIGHT BE SUKHOI-25(*)... SLOW THEM DOWN AS WELL!

(*) Single-seat, two-engine ground attack aircraft

GO THERE AT LOW ALTITUDE... FOUR OF THE MIGS THAT ARE LOOKING FOR YOU WILL BE ON YOUR VECTOR... CURRENTLY AT LEVEL 180(*)...

Approximately 19,000 ft altitude   NS34A

AT OSAN, BUCK IS KEEPING BUSY...

IT'S OUT OF THE QUESTION TO TRY AGAIN FOR NOW. I... WHAT IS IT, CORPORAL?

URGENT CONFIDENTIAL MESSAGE, SIR.

THE RC-135 IS REPORTING THAT THEY INTERCEPTED EXTREMELY ANGRY NORTH KOREAN RADIO EXCHANGES CONCERNING THE FAILURE TO CATCH OUR PILOT... COULD IT BE A LIE TO LEAD US INTO A TRAP?

I DON'T THINK SO, COLONEL. AND WONDERING ABOUT IT WON'T GET US ANYWHERE... WE HAVE TO HEAD BACK THERE TO MAKE SURE!

OKAY, DANNY... BUT WITH A SINGLE CHOPPER, READY TO TURN AROUND AT THE FIRST SIGN OF TROUBLE... DON'T FORGET THAT ALL THE DEFENCES ALONG THE DMZ ARE NOW ON ALERT. THE RISK IS SERIOUS...

MEANWHILE, TUMBLER HAS FOUND THE HELICOPTERS AND IS WORKING HARD TO GET THEM TO TURN AWAY, EITHER BY TURNING ON HIS FIRE-CONTROL RADAR BEHIND THEM, OR BY FIRING BURSTS FROM HIS GUN ACROSS THE NOSES OF THE LEAD AIRCRAFT...

PYTHON TWO, THE MIGS ARE HEADING YOUR WAY!...

NS34B

THEY'VE GOT TO KNOW WHERE I AM NOW... A LITTLE HELP WOULD BE WELCOME!... I HOPE SONNY GETS HERE SOON...

PYTHON FOUR, COVER PYTHON 2 WITH A RADAR THREAT TOWARDS THE MIGS THAT COULD GIVE HIM SOME TROUBLE... THEN YOU'LL SWITCH JOBS.

ON MY WAY, TUMB... HANG ON!

FURTHER SOUTH...

RATTLESNAKE, THIS IS ANACONDA... WE'RE DONE HERE. THE LAST OF OUR PERSONNEL ARE EMBARKING. WE'RE READY TO GO HOME!

NS35A

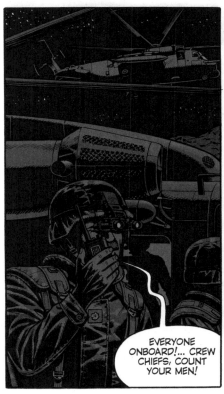

EVERYONE ONBOARD!... CREW CHIEFS, COUNT YOUR MEN!

FURTHER WEST, DICK'S SITUATION IS GETTING CRITICAL...

I CAN'T MAKE MYSELF KNOWN TO THE SUKHOI WITHOUT EXPOSING MYSELF TO THE MIGS... I'M GOING TO END UP GETTING SMOKED!

Francis Bergese

NS35B

WHILE TO THE NORTHEAST...

WITH TWO PEOPLE WE'RE GETTING SOMEWHERE... BUT WE'RE RUNNING LOW ON AMMO...

PYTHON TWO AND FOUR: FORGET THE CHOPPERS AND GO HELP PYTHON THREE... BEARING 2-6-0...

AT THE SAME INSTANT, OVER THE DMZ...

FLYING LOW INSIDE VALLEYS WILL KEEP US SAFE FROM MISSILES AND RADAR-GUIDED GUNS.

NS36A

BUT IT WON'T PROTECT US FROM LIGHT WEAPONS FIRE...

SOON AFTER, INDEED...

WE HAVE THE MEANS TO SHOOT BACK: THREE RAPID-FIRE MACHINE GUNS THAT CAN DO SOME DAMAGE... BUT ONLY IF THE SITUATION BECOMES CRITICAL... SO, WE HUNCH OUR SHOULDERS, KEEP OUR HEADS DOWN AND WAIT TILL IT'S OVER!

NS36B

ONLY 20 MILES AWAY, THREE F-22S ARE STRUGGLING TO SLOW THE ADVANCE OF SOME SUKHOI-25S WHILE EVADING NUMEROUS MIGS...

WE CAN'T GO ON LIKE THIS... THE RISKS HAVE GONE WAY PAST THE RED LINE... I'M BREAKING RADIO SILENCE...

OWLEYE FROM PYTHON TWO... THE SITUATION IS UNTENABLE!... FIND ANOTHER SOLUTION, AND FAST!

MAJ JERRY TUMBLER

NS36C

WHOA! TWO BIRDS JUST COLLIDED!

PYTHON THREE... I'M OKAY!

PYTHON FOUR, I'M OKAY... BUT WE CAN'T KEEP THIS UP!

PHEW!

PYTHON, WATCH DOG: FALL BACK UNDER STEALTH IMMEDIATELY ALONG THE PLANNED ROUTE!... YOU'VE DONE A GREAT JOB!... RATTLESNAKE AND ANACONDA ARE ABOUT TO GET BACK THROUGH THE LINES... OPERATION SNEAKY SERPENT IS A SUCCESS!

NS37A

TWELVE MINUTES LATER, THE 12 RAPTORS RENDEZVOUS WITH THE TANKER WAITING FOR THEM OVER THE YELLOW SEA...

HANG ON, BOYS! ANOTHER HOUR OF FLIGHT AND WE'LL HAVE A NICE BED AND UNLIMITED SLEEP!

WE CERTAINLY EARNED IT!

I HOPE PYTHON ONE WASN'T SCRATCHED TOO BADLY... WE'LL CALL WHEN WE LAND!

MEANWHILE...

YOU'RE SURE IT WAS THERE?

AFFIRMATIVE. WATCH DOG JUST CONFIRMED. THE AREA IS QUIET... YOU'RE A GO!

NS37B

NOBODY UNDER THE BRIDGE... NEITHER HERE NOR ON THE OTHER SIDE OF THE CANAL...

THIS GRATE IS UNLOCKED...

IT'S A SHAFT WITH AN ELBOW DOWNWARDS... HOLD ON TO MY FEET. I'LL CHECK IT OUT.

IT LEADS TO A DIMLY LIT TUNNEL ABOUT 15 FEET BELOW. YOU CAN HEAR THE DRONE OF A VENTILATION SYSTEM...

MAXWELL MUST HAVE CHOSEN THIS CONDUIT FOR HIS HIDING PLACE... IT'S POSSIBLE HE SLID DOWN THE ELBOW AND WAS UNABLE TO GET BACK UP...

NS38A

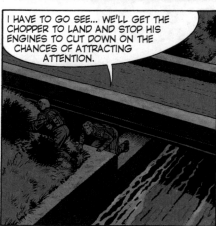

I HAVE TO GO SEE... WE'LL GET THE CHOPPER TO LAND AND STOP HIS ENGINES TO CUT DOWN ON THE CHANCES OF ATTRACTING ATTENTION.

SOON...

IF I'M NOT BACK IN 15 MINUTES, GO!... IF THE RC-135 GIVES YOU AN ALERT BEFORE THEN, DO THE SAME. WHETHER I FIND MAXWELL OR NOT, I'LL TURN MY BEACON ON WHEN I NEED TO BE PICKED UP!

GOOD LUCK, SIR. WE'LL DO OUR VERY BEST UNDER ANY CIRCUMSTANCES.

ALL YOU'LL HAVE TO DO WHEN YOU COME BACK IS GIVE THE ROPE SOME SLACK TO PUSH THE GRATE OPEN... I'LL STAY HERE UNTIL WE HAVE TO GO ANYWAY.

I'M AT THE END OF THE SHAFT...

NS38B

THE SHAFT WAS CLOSED BY THIS FAN. MAXWELL FELL ON IT, AND THE IMPACT TORE IT OFF... I'M ON THE RIGHT TRACK!

THE TUNNEL'S SLOPE FOLLOWS THE HILL'S. SO GOING DOWN IS GOING SOUTH... I IMAGINE THAT IF MAX WENT TO LOOK FOR AN EXIT, IT WOULD BE THIS WAY SO AS TO GET CLOSER TO THE BORDER.

I CAN HEAR THE SOUND OF AN ENGINE GETTING CLOSER... THE ROPE AND FAN MIGHT ATTRACT ATTENTION... I'LL PULL THEM INTO THIS DARK CORNER.

IT'S GONE QUIET AGAIN... TIME TO GO. IF I FIND MAX, THE EASIEST WAY WILL BE TO COME BACK HERE AND CLIMB BACK UP THE ROPE.

NS39A

HE'S GOT ALMOST A TWO-HOUR HEAD-START ON ME. IF HE'S NOT WOUNDED AND IF THIS TUNNEL IS LONG, HE COULD BE A LONG WAY AWAY!

I'D HEARD OF THOSE TUNNELS THAT WOULD ALLOW NORTHERN TROOPS TO COME UP IN THE SOUTH(*)... BUT I NEVER THOUGHT I'D HAVE A CHANCE TO DISCOVER ONE OF THEM!...

(*) True fact

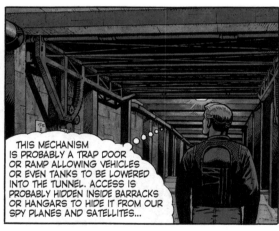

THIS MECHANISM IS PROBABLY A TRAP DOOR OR RAMP ALLOWING VEHICLES OR EVEN TANKS TO BE LOWERED INTO THE TUNNEL. ACCESS IS PROBABLY HIDDEN INSIDE BARRACKS OR HANGARS TO HIDE IT FROM OUR SPY PLANES AND SATELLITES...

AND BUCK RESUMES HIS RUN...

... SLOWING DOWN OFTEN TO LISTEN CAREFULLY FOR ANY PATROL VEHICLES...

FORTY-FIVE MINUTES LATER...

A CROSSROADS... THERE MUST BE SEVERAL TUNNELS RUNNING PARALLEL, AND THIS ALLOWS PASSAGE BETWEEN THEM...

NS39B

NO SUSPICIOUS NOISES, NO SURVEILLANCE CAMERAS IN SIGHT... I'M CROSSING!

MY COMPASS IS GIVING ME A SOUTHEAST HEADING... STILL GOOD.

DARN IT!

...!... DARN IT?!

MAX! IT'S DANNY!

BUCK?!... GOOD GRIEF! IF YOU HADN'T SPOKEN, I'D HAVE SLIT YOUR THROAT!... I CAN HARDLY SEE, AND I SURE WASN'T EXPECTING...

WE'LL SAVE THE CHIT-CHAT FOR LATER... WE HAVE TO GO BACK TO THE AIR SHAFT QUICKLY: I LEFT A ROPE THERE THAT'LL ALLOW US TO CLIMB BACK OUT.

NS40A

HOW ARE YOU FEELING?

I ATE MY RATIONS AND DRANK WATER FROM THE CANAL... I'M FINE!...

MY PROBLEM IS SIGHT... I CAN ONLY MAKE OUT BLURRY SHAPES, BUT IT'S GETTING BETTER...

LOOK OUT!

THEY WERE COASTING DOWN... WITH THEIR ENGINES AND LIGHTS OFF...

THEY TURNED THEM ON WHEN THEY MUST HAVE SEEN US!

Francis Bergèse

NS40B

42

A WOMAN!

WHAT'S GOING ON, BUCK?!

I'M STUCK... I DON'T KNOW WHAT TO DO, MAX... SHE'S SCARED... IF I MOVE, SHE SHOOTS... IF I LOWER MY GUN, SHE SHOOTS...

TALK TO HER!

I... UNDERSTAND LITTLE! YOU... PRISONERS ME!

ME NOT PRISONER YOU! IF YOU SHOOT AT MY FRIEND, ME SHOOT AT YOU!

YOU'LL GUIDE US. WE WON'T HURT YOU.

I GUIDE YOU... THERE!

NO! WE WANT TO GO THIS WAY!

THIS WAY NOT GOOD! TRUCK SOLDIERS MUST COME SOON... POSSIBLE LEAVE END TUNNEL... THAT WAY.

GOOD GRIEF! SHE'S PLAYING WITH US! PUT YOUR RIFLE TO HER HEAD AND MAKE HER TURN AROUND!

ME GO WITH YOU KOREA SOUTH... THAT WAY!

I THINK SHE MEANS IT, MAX! LET'S GO!

I'M WARNING YOU, GIRL: AT THE FIRST SIGN OF TROUBLE, I SLIT YOUR FRIEND'S THROAT!

YOU CAN!... SHE POLITICAL COMMISSAR... FRIEND NOBODY!

SOME 10 MINUTES LATER...

ARE WE THERE YET?

IT WAS LAST CROSSROADS!

OH, MAN! I SAW SOME LIGHTS DOWN THE LEFT TUNNEL!

ARE THOSE TRUCKS AHEAD?

N542A

THEY'RE APCS EQUIPPED WITH CHAIN FLAILS TO CLEAR MINEFIELDS!

IN THE FRONT ARE TWO BULLDOZERS!

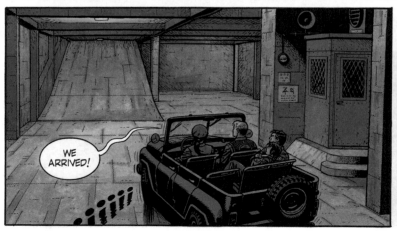

WE ARRIVED!

IT'S HERE TO MAKE EXIT EXPLODE!...

LISTEN!... A SIREN! THEY'VE SOUNDED THE ALARM BACK THERE!

N542B

SO?

I... TRY UNDERSTAND WHAT MUST DO...

THERE ARE VEHICLES APPROACHING! WHAT DO WE DO?

RELEASE YOUR PRISONER! IT MIGHT BUY US SOME TIME!...

GO! RUN BACK TO YOUR COUNTRYMEN!

더러운 돼지녀석!(*)

(*) Dirty American pigs!

쏘지마, 경찰이다!(*)

(*) Don't shoot! I am a political commissar!

TACATAC

AAARGH!

TAC

TONK

NS43A

TACATACATAC

PIAWN

BUCK! WHAT ARE YOU...?

BAOOM

BONG BOM TZING ZONK BWAM BAM

RHAAA!

POK

COME QUICK!

NS43B

FASTER, MAX!... FASTER!

PIAWW

I'M STUMBLING OVER ALL THIS RUBBLE!... WE'RE GONNA GET SHOT LIKE DUCKS IN A ROW!

LET ME WASTE SOME COMMIES BEFORE I CROAK!

TACATACA

NS44A

BAOOM

BROMBLOM
TZAK ZONK

WHAT THE...?

THERE WAS A CHARGE PLACED TO BLOCK THE TUNNEL IN CASE OF DISCOVERY OR COUNTER-ATTACK BY THE SOUTH KOREANS... FORTUNATELY, WITH A SELECTABLE TIME DELAY!

NS44B

THE BULLDOZERS WOULD HAVE CLEARED ACCESS TO THIS OPENING...

... AND THE APCS WOULD HAVE CLEARED A PATH THROUGH THE BORDER'S MINEFIELDS... WE'RE GONNA HAVE TO BE CAREFUL!

LET US GO FIRST, KID!... YOUR UNIFORM COULD MAKE MATTERS SERIOUSLY COMPLICATED!

꼼짝마!(*)

(*) Stay where you are!

NS44C

46

AMERICAN PILOTS! THERE ARE THREE OF US!

움직이지마! 지뢰밭이다!(*)

(*) Don't move! Minefield!

COME GET US!

THE PATH IS FAR! WE'LL HAVE TO REQUEST A HELICOPTER!

THAT SAME DAY, AROUND NOON...

AN AIRCRAFT COMING FROM NORTH KOREA IS CROSSING THE DMZ HEADING FOR SEOUL, SECTOR S-30!

WE HAVE AN F-16 PATROL CLOSE BY... VECTOR THEM FOR IDENTIFICATION AND WARNINGS!

SOON...

IT'S AN F-6(*)... ITS LANDING GEAR IS DOWN AS A SIGN OF SURRENDER!

BRING IT TO SEOUL AIR BASE!

(*) Chinese version of the Russian MiG-19

NS 45A

FIFTEEN MINUTES LATER...

I AM GENERAL YANG DONG-IN OF THE PEOPLE'S REPUBLIC OF KOREA AIR FORCE... I REQUEST POLITICAL ASYLUM!

THAT EVENING IN OKINAWA...

MY FRIENDS, I HAVE INFORMATION FOR YOU AS A CONCLUSION TO OUR OPERATION "SNEAKY SERPENT"...

THE NORTH KOREAN GENERAL YANG, WHO WAS RESPONSIBLE FOR THE MEDIA OPERATION CENTRED ON OUR DOWNED F-16, DEFECTED BEFORE HE COULD SUFFER THE CONSEQUENCES OF HIS FAILURE...

HE REVEALED HOW THE WHOLE OPERATION WAS SET UP... HOW THEIR INTELLIGENCE SERVICES HAD A KOREAN EMPLOYEE AT MAXWELL'S BASE MODIFY HIS NAVIGATION SOFTWARE, AND HOW THEY BLINDED HIM WITH A RADAR-GUIDED LASER GUN OF THEIR CONSTRUCTION...

Francis Bergese

NS45B

NO DOUBT IT WAS A BITTER PILL TO SWALLOW FOR THE NORTHERN PROPAGANDISTS, WHO HAD TO EXPLAIN THEMSELVES IN FRONT OF THE ASSEMBLED WORLD PRESS, SINCE ALL THEY COULD SHOW THEM WAS A PODIUM ERECTED IN FRONT OF AN EMPTY CLEARING!

NOW THAT THEY KNOW THEIR WHOLE SCHEME WAS GIVEN AWAY BY ONE OF ITS MAIN ACTORS, IT'S SAFE TO ASSUME THAT THE JOURNALISTS WERE ONLY SUBJECTED TO A VIOLENT ANTI-WESTERN RANT...

... AND THAT OUR INCURSION—WHICH THEY DIDN'T MANAGE TO PREVENT—WILL BE BURIED!... I'M SURE NEITHER THEIR GOVERNMENT NOR OURS WILL WANT TO SEE THEIR SCHEMES OR WEAKNESSES EXPOSED IN THE OPEN!

IS THERE ANY NEWS ON OUR LITTLE SOLDIER?

SHE'S CURRENTLY BEING DEBRIEFED BY KOREAN ARMY INTELLIGENCE. SHE'LL PROBABLY BE DRAFTED IN: HER KNOWLEDGE WILL BE VERY USEFUL!

CUTE?

VERY!

STUCK IN A TUNNEL WITH A PRETTY GIRL... WHY DOESN'T THIS SORT OF THING HAPPEN TO ME?!

NS46A

TONIGHT, MAXWELL, BUCK AND I ARE LEAVING ON THE REGULAR C-17(*) FOR HAWAII. MAXWELL WILL UNDERGO SURGERY THERE. THE CHANCES ARE GOOD THAT HIS VISION WILL RETURN TO NORMAL.

(*) US Air Force four-engine cargo plane

TOMORROW, YOU OTHERS, THE THREE AVAILABLE F-22S, WILL HEAD BACK TO YOUR BASE AT EDWARDS, WITH A STOPOVER IN HAWAII. BUCK'S PLANE WILL BE DISMANTLED AND SHIPPED BACK HOME ON A "GALAXY"(*)...

(*) The US Air Force's largest transport aircraft

THAT'S RIGHT! THE BEST AREN'T ALWAYS WHO YOU'D THINK!

just call me Targy

THE END

The author would like to thank for their friendly help: Jean-Marc Brûlez, Hubert Cance, Yvan Fernandez, Patrick Guérin, Colonel (Ret. USAF) Robert D. Haley, Claude Magnan, Jean-Marc Tanguy, Stéphane "Steph" Pierre-Tumelaire, and especially Mr Song Jung-Chil, cultural and press attaché at the Korean Embassy in France. Colours are by Frédéric Bergèse.